RED SAILS ON THE STOUR

THE ORIGINAL STORY BY
JONATHAN WAINWRIGHT

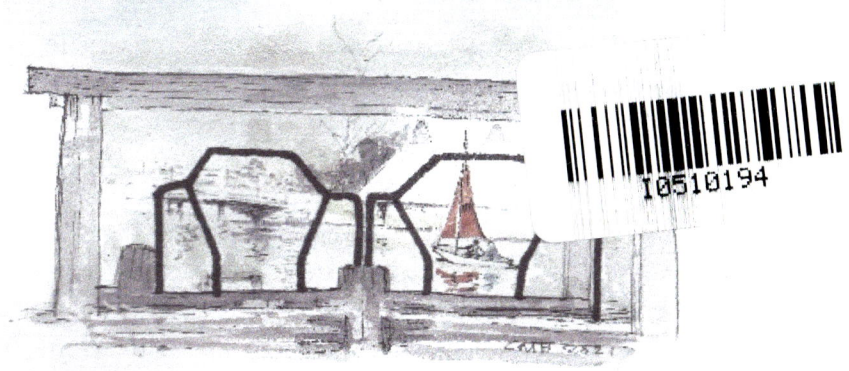

RECENT ILUSTRATIONS BY
COLIN HART

FOREWORD

This little gem was written over two score years ago at a time when the River Stour Trust was in its infancy and full of the hopes of a shining and rejuvenated future for the navigation. It is a good-humoured account of the difficulties in trying to do something that, at the time, was considered almost impossible. Or at the very least foolhardy but is it not the British way to love and venerate eccentricity?

The Dedham Vale, beautiful in its own right, is but a small part of the greater Stour Valley offering much to one who will search it out. May I quote Sir Alfred Munnings writing in 1957, "In spite of the shattering noise of planes in the sky today, peace can still be found by the banks of the Stour."

Perhaps this publication will help to rekindle the public interest in what is an incredibly beautiful yet secluded river that offers an escape from this jaded world for the lucky few that can take to a small craft and follow the example contained herein. Let us not forget that without the navigation there would not have been any locks or lighters for John Constable to paint and no derelict lighters at Dedham for Munnings to do likewise.

Jim Lunn
Archivist and Trustee
River Stour Trust

INTRODUCTION

The original sailing trip took place on 21-22 June 1978. We embarked on a weekend trip down the river Stour from Sudbury to Manningtree. We attempted this in a small dinghy 'Mirror 10' – REG 32722.

Jonathan Richard Wainwright and I first met in 1974, when local government reorganisations were taking place. I had hoped to head the expanded Architect's section, but this was not to be. Jon came for interview for the principal post, and I was asked to show him around the newly refurbished facilities. "Could you work with him?" asked the boss man afterwards. "Yes" I replied.

Jon and I soon formed a friendship, arguing at times, but always parting friends – usually after a lunchtime visit to the Limes in Needham Market.

I had several more years' experience in architecture than Jon, however he had the qualifications.

He also had other talents. His main passion was his gaffed rigged Morecambe Bay Prawner, the Deva. This had been purchased by his late father. Jon's book, **Only So Many Tides**, describes his attachment to Deva, and a journey across England – from the Mersey on the West coast to the Humber on the East Coast and on to Tollesbury in Essex.

Jon and has family eventually settled at Mistley on the Essex side of the Stour.

Here he became the secretary of the Old Gaffer's Association. Jon was an athlete – swimmer, runner, and could sink a pint or two! He was also hooker at Bury St Edmunds Rugby Club.

However, Jon, like his father before him, had underlying health problems and associated major surgery. He tried to keep fit and we would swim a mile together several times a week.

Jon retired and continued to sail in the Deva. Prophetically his last tide was on 22 July 2007. He died, tiller in hand, at night, crossing the North Sea on his way to meet sailing friends in Holland.

Thanks, Jon, for great sailing experiences. This little story of our unique sail down the Stour is one of them.

My original intention was to use a laptop, and digitally add the Mirror to the scenes. I could not master the technology!

Much of the river is remote and photographs could only be taken at crossing points. These were used as the basis for little water colour sketches.

This was my first attempt at water colour having attended a short course at Denman College earlier.

I hope you enjoy them.

Colin Hart   *April 2021*

LIST OF SKETCHES

Acknowledgements:

Margaret Wainwright for allowing' Jon's story to be retold. My brother, Phil, for retyping. Grandson Jack for editing. Andy Abbott Photography for the cover photographs. And to Joy for accompanying me on return visits to The Stour.

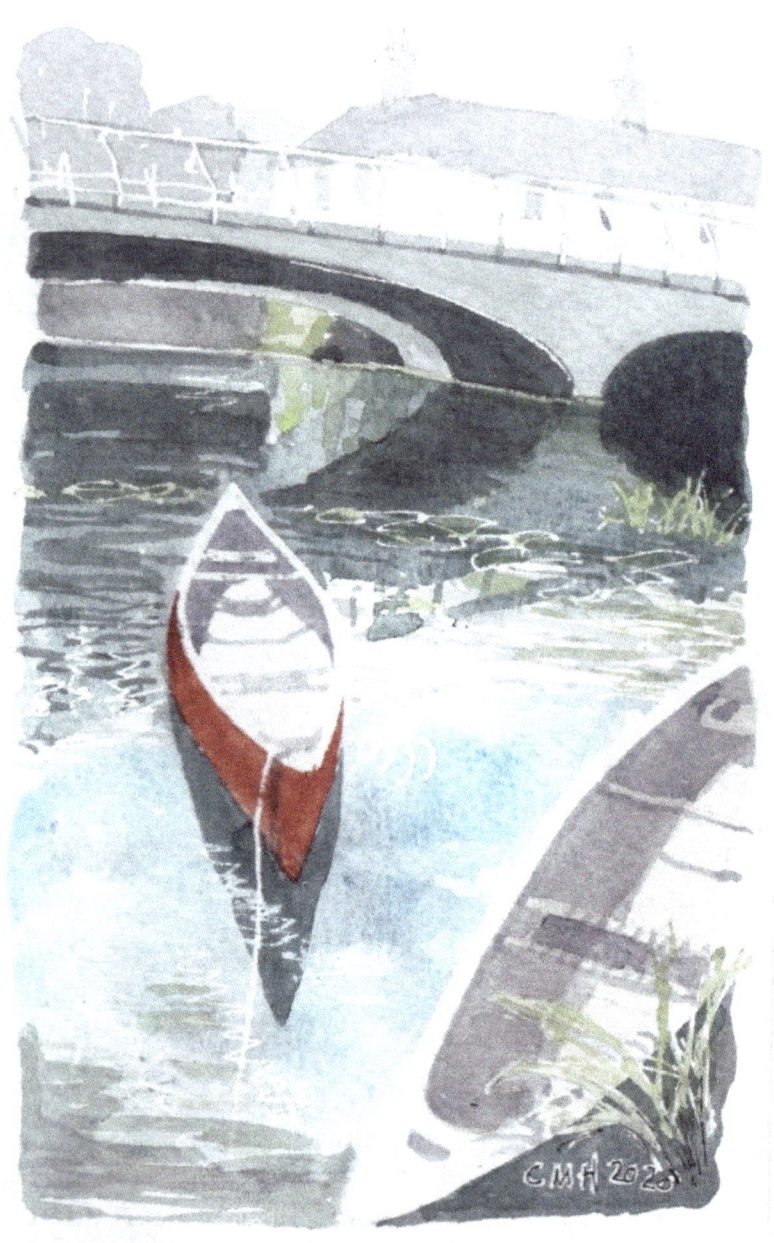

RED SAILS ON THE STOUR

BY JONATHAN WAINWRIGHT

Any visitor to Britain's coastline will see thousands of sailing dinghies underway on a weekend. Dinghies just like my little Mirror 10 – of which there are over 60,000. However, it amazes me that well over half these boats are just racing round little triangular courses, pushing rules of the road to the limit. Why cannot these people just be happy sailing for sailings sake – is it because boats have become so efficient that they are boring? I do not know the answer to that one, but to me a sailing boat is also a delightful means of transport from one place to another. I was incredibly surprised to find at my local sailing club that no-one had sailed the upper reaches of the Stour, but I suppose that there are very few rivers which are sailed in this country.

Thus, apart from being a challenge to be the first sailing boat down the old Stour navigation, I thought it would be a remarkably interesting trip down one of East Anglia's most beautiful rivers.

The preparations for the voyage were minimal. The boat's rigging was modified slightly. The kicking strap purchase was used as a forestay tackle. A tapping lift was rigged to the boom. Camping gear, anchor and warps, an inflatable boat roller, a bottle of whisky, and the boat was ready.

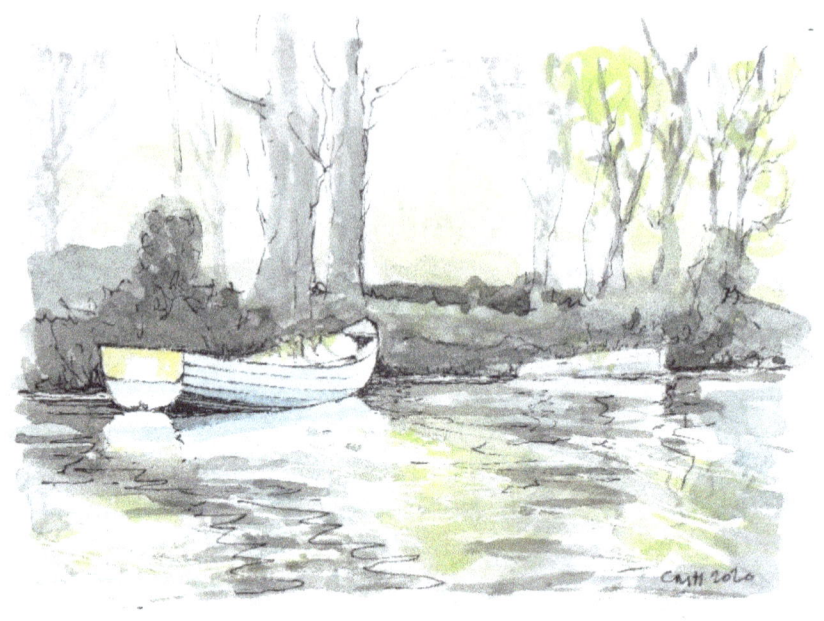

In fact, the wind took us to our first port of call at Friars Meadow, still in Sudbury without a sail being set. Here we completed the rigging and posed for photographs for the Press.

The press conference being completed, we started the voyage properly at 10:20 and in fine style with a quartering wind. The river here is broad and deep, and to my mind perfectly adequate for dinghy sailing and racing on a larger scale – there are well used stretchers on the Thames and Broads which are no better. (At this point I think I should mention that I have had a truly little sailing dinghy experience (neither has my partner), most of my sailing being done in a septenegerian prawner at sea. The contrast between this and a modern dinghy on an inland river must be appreciated.

Sweeping passed the willow trees, a fine rate of knots was not to last, as Cornard weir loomed up on the starboard bow – very cautiously we lowered sail and glided up the Mill cut and prepared for our first portage. In comparison with a canoe, we were not able to use landing stages provided by the trust. Our boat loaded up with camping gear, food and whisky was no light weight, and we did not wish to unload at every portage. Our technique was to improve considerably as the voyage went on, but the basic principles were as follows:

Unless closing a weather shore, we would lower mainsail and jib, and cast the anchor onto the bank, preferably where there was a good thickness of grass. The centre plate and rudder would be unshipped, and the craft hauled to the bank. The inflatable roller would be blown up and with a lift on the bow and a heave, we would be land-borne. With good thick grass the roller could be dispensed with and we would launch stern first in the new level, rig centered board and rudder, and set sail. Paddles were only used occasionally to push off from the bank.

The portage at Cornard, an easy one, took about twenty minutes – towards the end we were taking five. Practice makes perfect.

Unfortunately, at Cornard the wind was dead ahead, as it would be all the way to Henny. The current was of little help, and we could make but ten yards per tack. Weeds and lilies were a slight problem when rounding up, but generally far less than they would have been to a power boat or canoe.

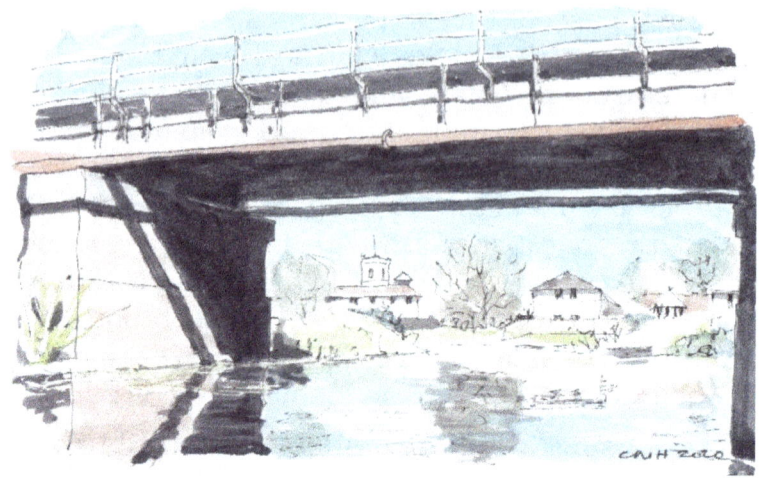

Before leaving Cornard we did run aground quite painfully at times, through having to use the whole width of the river for tacking. However, this very difficult reach taught us new techniques in dinghy sailing. Instead of helmsman and crew swapping around each tack and stepping over the dunnage and each other as is traditional, we found that staying where we were was far more restful. Rounding up was different – at sea it is imperative to get moving on the new tack as soon as possible. On the river it paid to sail the boat almost into the bank and the water pressure between it and the lee-bow eased the bow round, along the bank for a length or two and as the boat began to stall a nudge of the helm took her onto the new tack.

About half-way between Cornard and Henny it began to rain, and the antics of two men donning oilskins on a 10-foot dinghy tacking across a 30-foot river must have appeared amusing. More worrying than this was causing loss of drinking time.

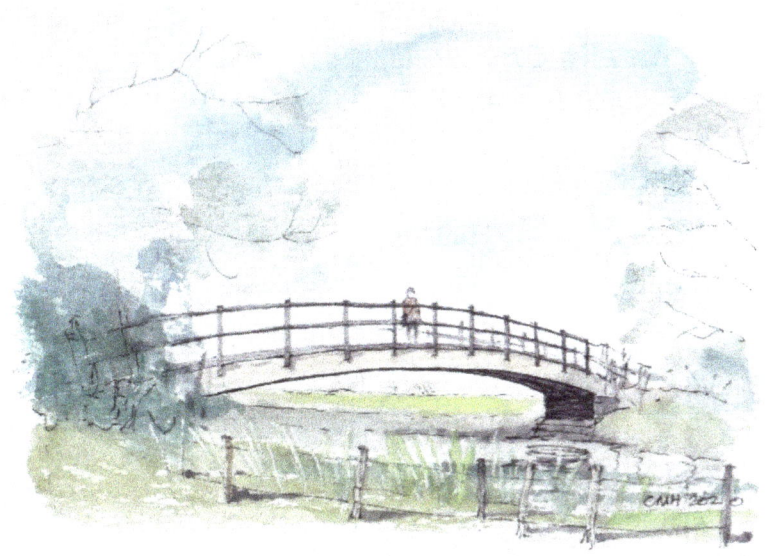

The river up to Henny Street was in surprisingly good condition, navigationally speaking, and had the wind been favourable it would have taken only half an hour or so to reach the hostelry from Sudbury. However, the journey took us over one and a half hours!

Despite the setbacks of wind and weather, we were in fine spirits as the real ale reached those parts where lagers will never do! It was an indescribable experience sailing through the middle of East Anglia. The trees, the wildlife, the utter peace of sail – it was fantastic. Even had we to give up at Henny Street, it was worth it.

We portaged the weir and lowered the boat into the river. The footbridge required the mast to be lowered, another technique which was to reach horrifying perfection before the trip was over!

We had been warned that the river would deteriorate in condition, but from a sailing point of view the wind was a little easier and the current faster.

Shalford Meadow weir came up rather suddenly. You have to remember that a sailing boat with the wind travels much faster than a cruising canoe or even a motor boat at times, and you can bet the wind is both strong and free just before a weir!

The banks along this reach were much higher than before, so although the wind was quite strong, being cross-river in direction it caught the sails on occasions only, giving rather leap-frog progress.

Each bend in the river was a complete surprise to us, and Pitmire was no exception. The rain gave over to hot sun, and in the dense vegetation and trees, it was just like a jungle in Malaya. In fact, we could not resist creeping up to a Pill Box and shouting "Alright, you can come out now – the war's over – we won!" However, if a German or Japanese came out now, and saw the relative states on the victorious and defeated countries, he would have to do some research to convince himself that his country did not win the war!

A diesel railcar clattered over a bridge and brought us back to our senses, as we hacked our way through the undergrowth to study a way round the obstruction. The lock chamber still exists, as does a real lock lintel! However there did not seem an easy way round, so having lunched (and topped up with a couple of slugs of whisky) we launched just below the weir. The river below was shallow and restricted with consequent fast current.

There were also cross currents where water was cutting through the old lock chamber. We had to paddle this short stretch to the railway bridge before we could set sail again.

Shortly after the Pitmire lock site we nearly killed an angler through shock! In fact, it was interesting to note the reactions of the few people and many animals who saw us. With all the twists and bends in the river there was little notice we could give of our silent arrival. Despite the reputation of hostility anglers have towards boats, everyone we passed nodded in shocked salutation as the Mirror ghosted by. Cattle on the other hand followed us in herds, whilst swans glared and hissed if we sailed too close to their young.

From Pitmire down, one was much more aware of being in a valley. The river twists and turns so much that on occasions we thought we were sailing into hills, only to find that the river made 360 degree turns in the nick of time! From a sailing point of view, it was tricky a times. After a struggle of a beat, we would find the river suddenly turn in our favour – speed would quadruple, and we would just about have time for a quick slug then the river would turn foul again!

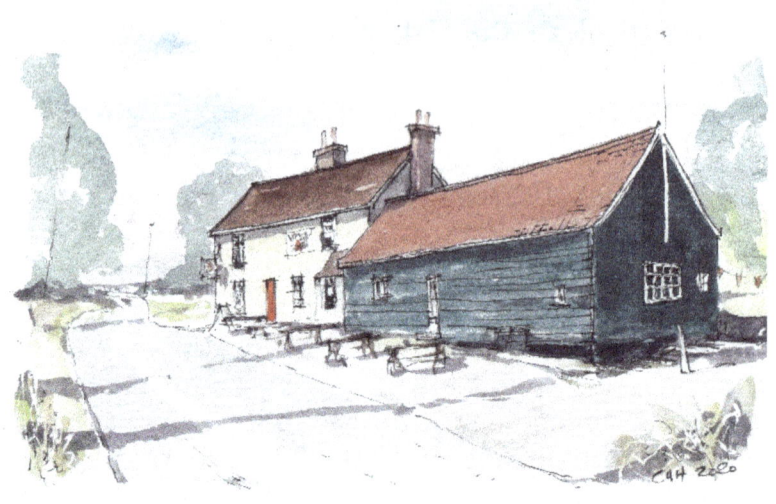

However, once we had portaged round Lamarsh weir (where we shipped much water over the stern through getting too close to the weir), the wind was more often in our favour than not. At one point, just after Lamarsh we could not see how the river was going to end as the Essex and Suffolk hills met – it was an optical illusion, but we seemed to be going uphill!

More rain came down as we approached Bures, which took away much of the wind. Then as we rounded into the last reach before Bures itself, we saw that the Suffolk County Council were in the middle of repairing the bridge, and the whole opening was crisscrossed with scaffolding.

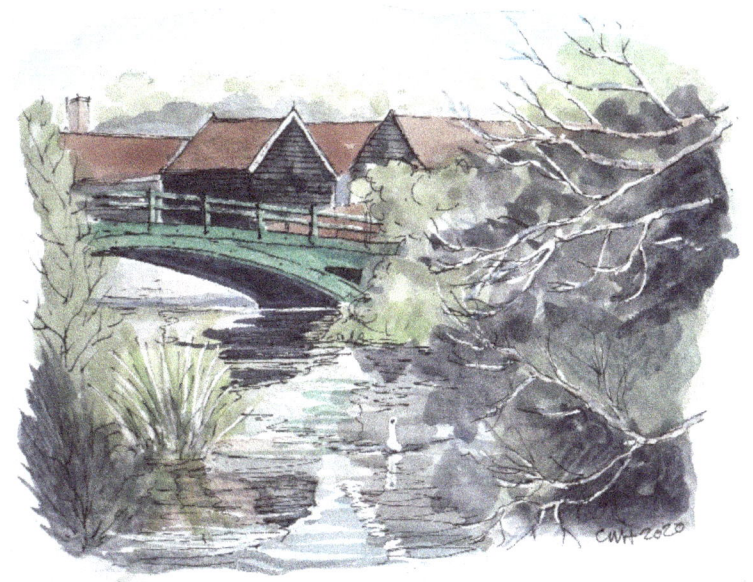

I was all for unbolting this thoughtless obstruction to navigation, but my partner persuaded me to un-rig the mast and by lying flat we went under with inches to spare. Bures took a long time to navigate as the wind, which should have been favourable as the river turns easterly at this point, disappeared completely. Probably the backs of the several riverside houses blanketed most of it. Bures was the first place since Sudbury where we saw any other boats, many dwellings having small landing stages.

As we left the village the wind picked up again, although only in a light air. There was a rather dangerous obstruction in the middle of the river, which could have been nasty if we had not swerved at the last minute.

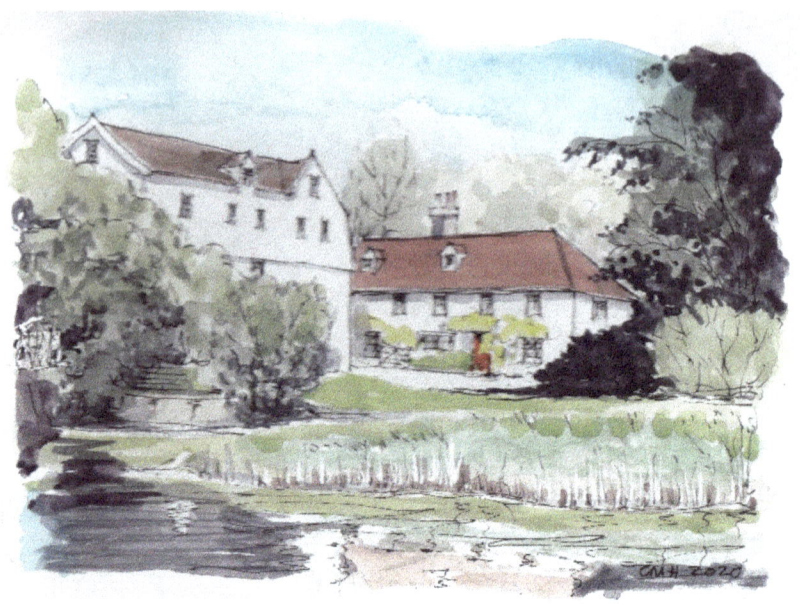

Bures Mill was a difficult portage. We had to man-handle the boat down a ditch and under a footbridge which had a vicious looking stake protruding underneath. By careful movement, an inch at a time, the Mirror squeezed through.

The river from the mill was shallow, high banked and reeded, but to compensate the wind was fair and the current of the swollen stream strong. Often it was quite exhilarating to sweep through the reeds at six knots, steering for where there was room for the yard and room for the beat. At one or two places the boom tangled with the reeds and the current threw us right into the vegetation.

Generally, the river improved as we neared Wormingford Mill. There seemed only one way through the forest which divided the river from the mill pool, and had a poacher seen a sailing boat being man-handled through leaves and bushes he would have known that Englishmen are mad.

As the guidebook says this is a uniquely beautiful part of the Stour, the willows enclosing the mill pool giving a fantastic atmosphere of sound and enclosure.

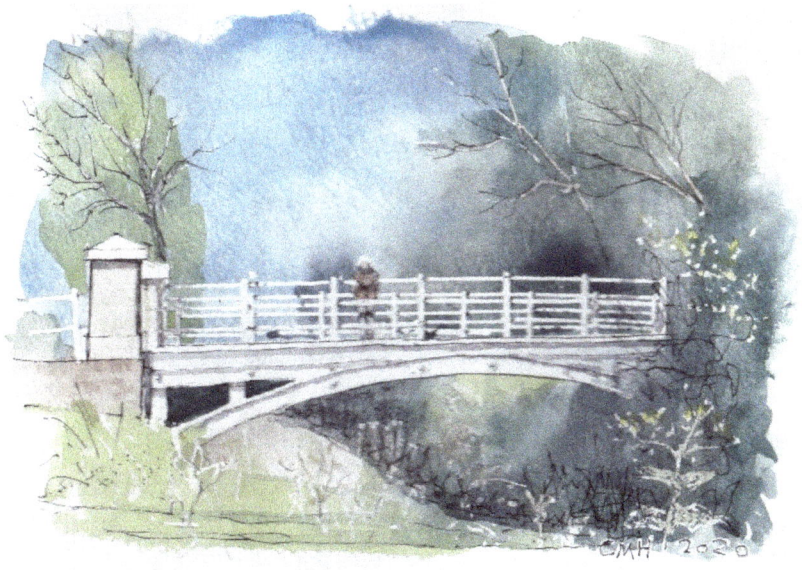

Having shot the bridge at Wormingford, we continued our way. We were beginning to become hungry at this stage, as it was well into the evening. However, whilst the failing breeze was still favourable and progress reasonable, we thought we must try and make Nayland before we moored for the night.

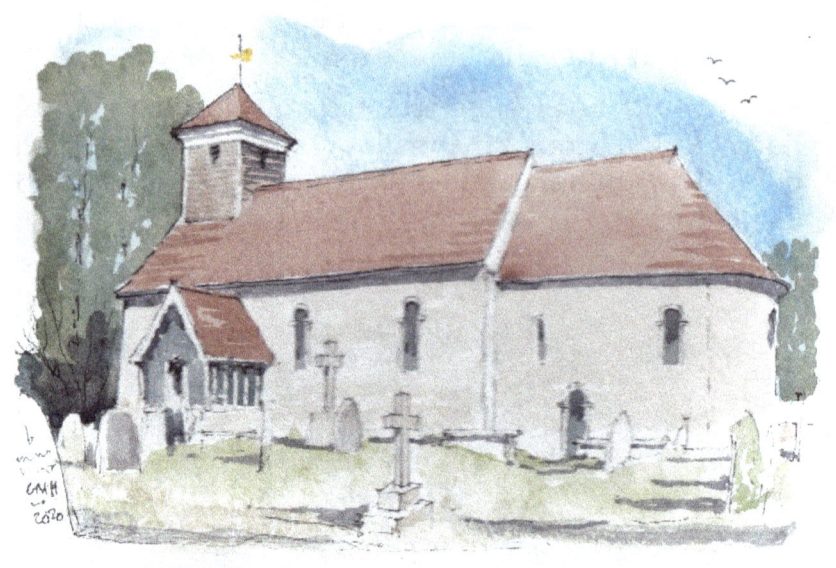

The river down to Wissington Mill was in good condition, but there was one reach which was wooded, leaving gaps of less than a foot between tree branches for the mast to pass through.

Wissington Mill is probably the most picturesque part of the river, but the weir gave an exceedingly difficult portage on account of the height of the banks. We did contemplate pitching our tent here, but there was no suitable site nor accessible hostelry.

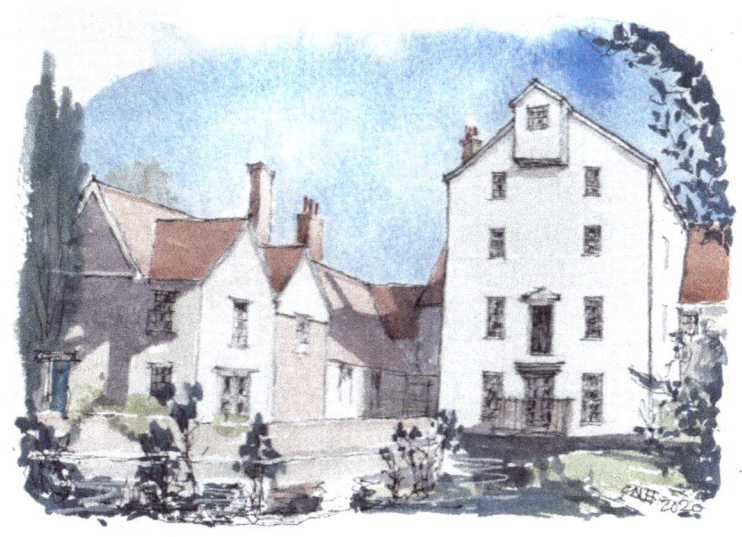

We carried the last of the evening breeze towards Nayland but were nearly foiled by the relief channel works and had to claw back to where the river proper turned off. The culvert under the A134 was negotiated quickly, but I had to chuckle at the effect the sight of a sailing boat on a collision course with the road must have had on motorists. This would be followed by a disappearing act as the craft shot down a rat hole and a further surprise as the red sails suddenly shot up again on the other side of the road.

On the Suffolk side of the river there was a large area of common land, so we had arrived, our sleeping bags were soaking wet. It was our own fault for omitting to cover them in polythene. In the event we put the polythene in the damp sleeping bags!

Whilst at Nayland, the Stour Trust president, Mr. Francis Batten introduced himself to us.

He had spotted the red sails gliding through the fields by his home and had followed us down. He said he would try and arrange for Flatford lock to be opened, and we told him that we should be at Flatford at about 3 – 4 pm.

After a few pints in Nayland we retired to our polythene bags to awake next morning in a very damp condition. However, a quick jog round the common and the addition of extra layers of clothing made us warm enough to enjoy breakfast.

Early Morning 22 June 1978

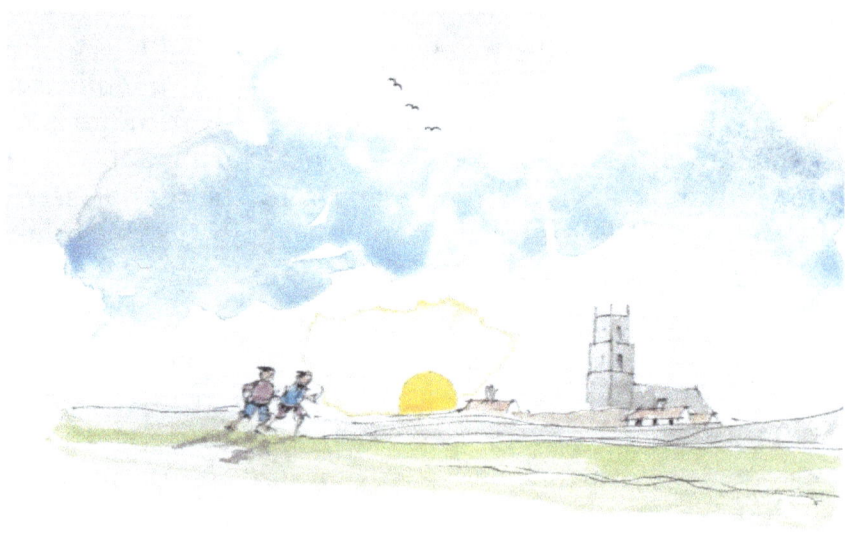

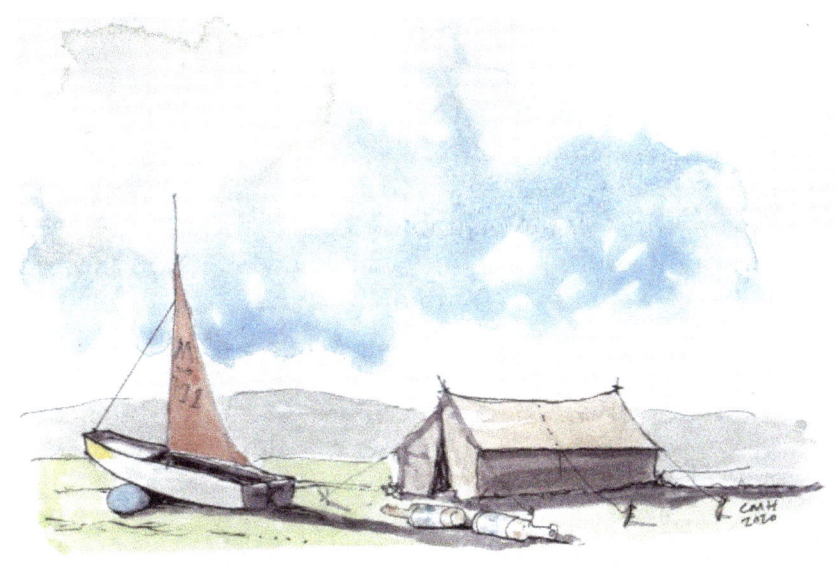

We set sail at 08:30 am on the second leg in a spanking breeze and sailed quickly passed the backs of houses. A lady from one of them came rushing out saying "Hey, it's the first I've seen a sailing boat on the river". Proudly we replied, "Yes ma'am, we're bound for Manningtree" only for her to shout, pointing behind us "You cannot go any further you know, there's a weir!". We turned round just as the boat was about to nose-dive over a waterfall!

Luckily, the obstruction was on the lee side of the boat and we were able to spin round into the wind away from the thundering weir. The portage at Nayland was quite a strenuous one, crashing through nettles and brambles and there was a strong current to launch into on the lower pound.

The river between the Nayland lock site and bridge was very restricted and shallow, although the rainfall had swollen it sufficiently to enable us to sail.

The trees took a bit of missing in the strong current, but the wind was sufficient to give us steerage way. We lowered the mainsail only on approaching the Nayland bridge, reckoning that it was high enough to take the mast – we reckoned incorrectly by two inches, and had to lower the mast very quickly! This error caused us to get in a spin right under the bridge, and in avoiding a jammed tree branch, we made a mess of setting sail, nearly demolishing the landing stage by the Anchor inn.

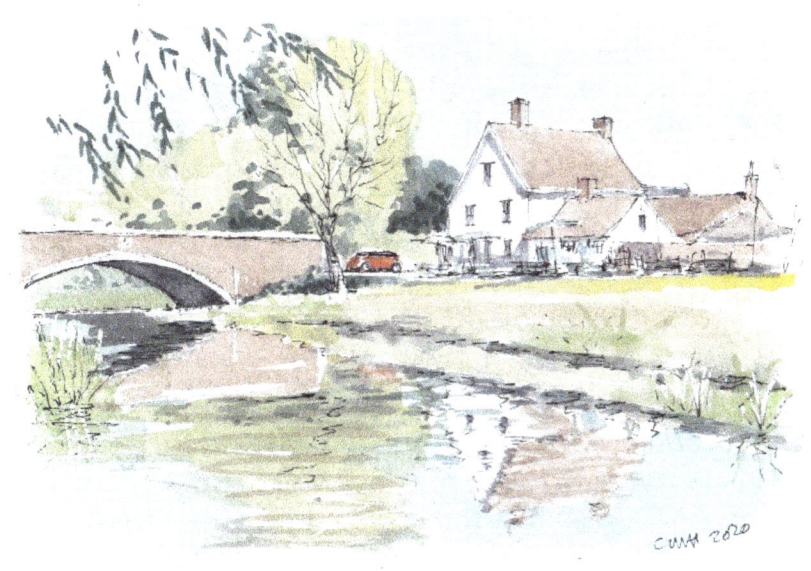

However, the boat was soon on a steady course, just to reach the next series of rapids. We took these in fine style with the following wind, swishing and swerving passed shallows, reeds and sandbanks.

Then horror of horrors we rounded a bend at a speed of six or seven knots to face a complete willow tree which had obviously had only just crashed across the whole river.

With an emergency jibe we sheered into a sandbank which stopped us short of disaster by a good foot or so. The unexpected portage completed, we lowered into the fast current again. Gradually the water became calmer and more stately progress resumed.

On this reach we had more trouble with nesting swans as the river was narrow and the wind often blanketed by trees. We had a job avoiding these beautiful unfriendly creatures and were lucky not to be attacked. However, the red sails must have kept them at bay, as they must have appeared like the wings of a monster bird of prey! When the wind was clear and the Mirror took off pandemonium broke out as ducks took off squawking, rats scuttling back into their holes – clearly few craft navigated this stretch.

The willow trees gradually gave way to other species and the river straightened up in the final run up to Boxted mill. This mill, now in private ownership, had been beautifully converted and its owner had laid both sides of the river to lawn. There was also a boat house.

We passed a signpost saying, "canoes this way", but we moored some distance nearer the weir. After all, portaging a lightweight canoe is one matter, but a laden sailing vessel is another kettle of fish. Colin went off to scout out a launching spot, whilst I prepared the dinghy for portage.

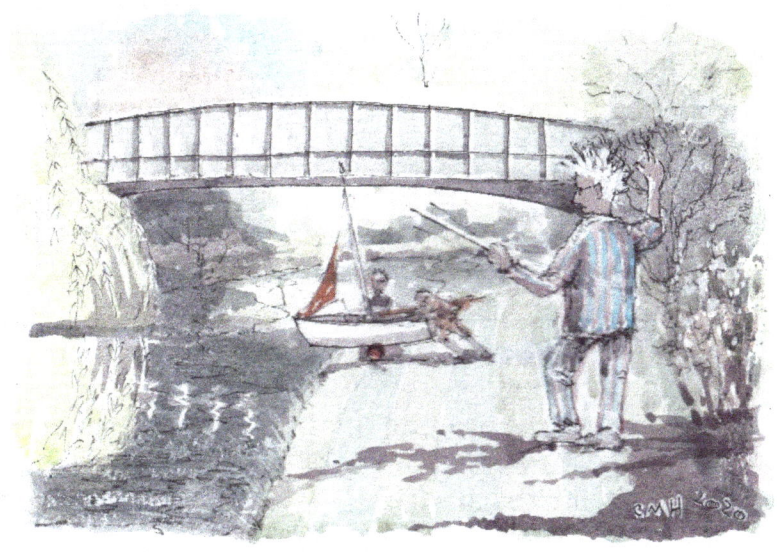

He returned to find a fuming riparian owner in his pyjamas giving me a dressing- down on the fact that it was his land I was navigating across and I had no right to do so. "Where were the locks?" he said – I suppose he had a point, hence my desire to take a short cut across his lawn and orchard!

However, it was a rather funny argument. Interspersed with telling me off, hc kepl saying he could not believe how we had sailed from Sudbury – he could not even believe his eyes that a sailing boat was moored to his lawn!

In the end he said that just this once, without prejudice, he would allow us to cross his property. In future we should ring him up, and gain permission to use the canoe path.

With wry smiles on our faces Colin and I dropped the Mirror into the mill pool (with the boat roller, we did not damage the lawn). We paddled across the pool and did not set sail until after the road bridge. The water was very shallow, with one or two projecting stones to hole the unwary.

The river appeared to cut right into the land with many trees clinging to the bank. Shortly after the Langham lock site the Langham gauging weir appeared. We closed the bank, looking desperately for a portage point – the guidebook says it can be portaged either side, but the banks are steep sided and about twelve feet or more high. We hurled the anchor up on the bank in the end and scrambled up to survey the river situation. It looked useless, if not hopeless. There was no way we could haul the Mirror up the bank without unloading all the gear, and there were precious few places where there was enough water to drop her in lower down.

Clearly there had to a way, for to sail back to Boxted Mill was out of the question for reasons not nautical! However, it would take a long time and a lot of effort. Colin, who had done a fair amount of canoeing could see no problem – shoot the weir!

After considering ways of easing down the flumes, we decided to do it canoe style in the end. Centre board and rudder were shipped, the sails stowed, and we set off, with my heart in my mouth, if not my crew's!

It was the first time I had shot a weir, and it was not as bad as I thought.

As we hit the white water we paddled like fury to keep her direction true – a degree either way and we could have caught a rock or the back eddy. The surf burbled at gunwale height as we dropped down and water poured through the centreboard casing, but we were through.

Our troubles were not over with this reach, however, as the water was so shallow that we had to get our feet wet and guide the boat round. A swan gave us a piece of her mind, but soon we were sailing again in about ten inches of water, occasionally touching the center plate.

The heavily wooded stretch began to clear, and the water deepened. With alarm we heard running water, but this was only the sound of the water authority works. We passed a party of Scouts standing on the abutments of the collapsed Langham bridge. Their map was not up to date, and they had doubts about fording the river. We told them to go a little way up stream where a crossing could be made easily.

The river now improved considerably, and good progress was made all the way to Stratford, except for one short reach which gave some tacking. There was one corner which took six tacks to negotiate, where a twisting wind and an overhanging tree foiled us completely. A small, heavily laden sailing boat tends to go sideways until its sails start to draw properly, and an awkward combination of wind and obstruction proved this point emphatically!

We reached Stratford lock, but opted to continue down the mill stream, as the lock cut was overgrown. Even the mill stream became heavily treed, forcing us to drop mast and sail for the last hundred yards or so. We found a portage point where a relief sluice passed under the footbridge by the mill site.

Having launched the boat on a new level, we decided it was time for liquid refreshment, having had lunch on the sail down.

At the third pub we struck lucky with the ale and having sank a couple of well-deserved pints returned to our ship.

The river immediately after Stratford Mill was heavily treed, and with the wind direction fine on the starboard bow, it took some negotiation. We sailed passed Le Talbooth with several score of spectators watching. As is usual in such circumstances the wind suddenly, without so much of a warning went round 180 degrees and blew us into a bush. I heard one gent remark to his friend "I say, have you ever read Michael Green's book, The Art of Course Sailing!".

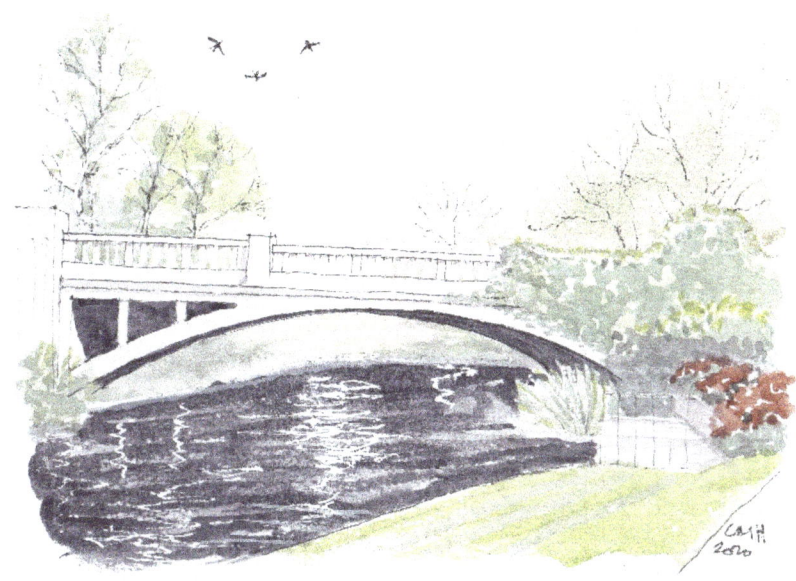

With hurt pride we sailed under the old bridge with scandalized main and fors'l, but in much better spirits we set full sail under the new A12 bridge and shot out in fine style.

This achievement of sailing under the A12 must surely rank with Rounding the Horn backwards or other feats of maritime history!

Most lovers of the Stour will know the reach down to Dedham. The open Suffolk side appeared to be lower than the river – perhaps this is an optical illusion. The boat sailed fast down this reach, which is in good navigation condition, and we soon arrived at Dedham Lock. This was the most difficult portage to arrange, although the guidebook says, "It is easily accomplished on the left-hand bank".

There is a gentle slope to lower the dinghy down, and the path down the left bank passed the Lockkeeper's cottage is too narrow for anything other than a canoe.

In the event we unshipped all our gear and lowered the boat into the old lock chamber, aided by three lads with canoes on the lower section. We drifted through the road bridge and had trouble rigging the boat, aggravated further by three hire boats ramming us! However, once rigged, the wind took a hold and we shot down to Flatford. Even the well-handled rowing boats could manage half our speed, and some desperate instructions to other less well-handled boats were needed to avoid collision. As it was, several boats took to the banks in fear, and I must apologise for inconvenience thus caused!

The wind eased as we approached Flatford bridge. Very few people seemed to notice anything strange about a sailing vessel on the river, all mad keen on Constable Culture. In my view it is a tragedy that tourism is concentrated at Flatford.

The Stour is steeped in culture at several other places and is beautiful throughout its length. If only the authorities and tourist organisations could get together and open the river to the visitor throughout its length – a proper tow path would be a start!

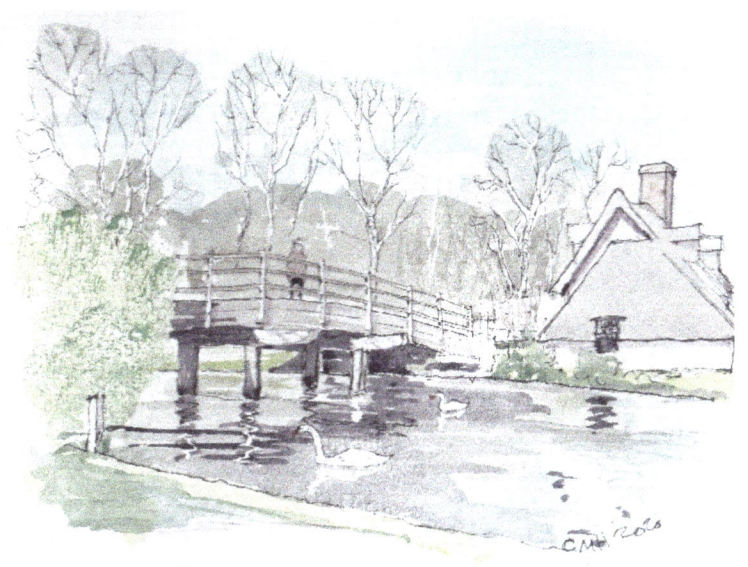

We had afternoon tea at Flatford as we waited to see if Mr. Bailey was available to open the lock. As it turned out it was in vain – it was a pity that we could not have arranged the matter more positively, but the voyage was very much a last minute affair, and it is difficult to sail a dinghy to schedule over uncharted waters!

After an hour's wait, during which my wife and children visited me with terrifying stories of rats invading our home, we portaged into the penultimate level.

As at Dedham the portage would have been difficult without the help of several canoeists.

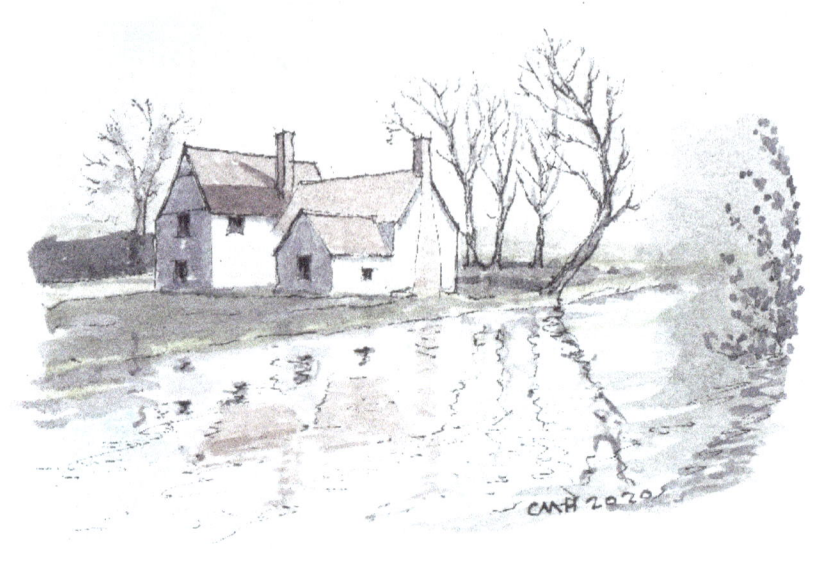

Just for old times' sake we made a short board in front of the mill and buildings, hoping my wife would take a photograph, but she disappeared in a throng owing to troubles with the children.

The final length of the navigation must have been done at record speed – the two miles or so to Cattawade taking less than twenty minutes. The sluices just below Flatford confused me – a change of level I had not reckoned on! However, the river suddenly turned to port and we went screaming round. On many stretches the strong breeze gave us planing speed, and the banks either side were blurred. Before I could say "c...t, there's a bridge at Brantham Lock site!" the mast and sail were over me and I did not even see the wretched obstruction.

Colin's sense of timing on the rigging was ranking on the mischievous and was downright criminal as we tore at the Cattawade culvert.

I knew we were not going to make it, I swerved one way then the other – the culvert headwall was too close – the mast would have to go rather than the hull – I shut my eyes........

I came to with Colin chuckling away - "Why did you panic?" I swear he could not have lowered the mast until two millimetres away from the culvert!

We drifted through the culvert and old Cattawade Bridge – surely the new one could have been better designed. I did hear that someone at the County tried to design a better one, but was out pointed on cost – surely a disgraceful situation in an area of outstanding natural beauty?

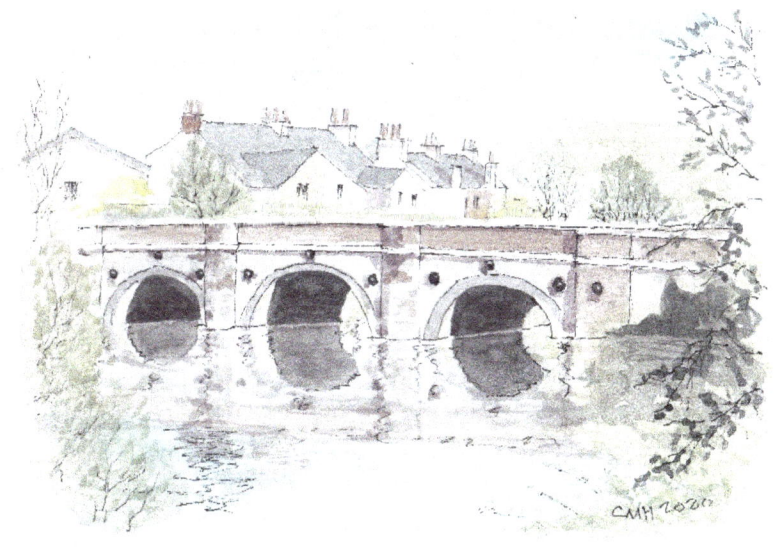

But the greatest disgrace was to come in the form of the Cattawade barrage.

This must rank as one of bureaucracy's greatest indifferences to those who value an Englishman's right to navigate the waters of his heritage.

In terms of vast amounts of money used – my money as tax and rate payer incidentally – the extra–over cost of a lock in lieu of an elaborate sluice chamber would be insignificant. The hidden benefits to the community of a working navigation would far outweigh this. Someone somewhere has "got it in" for individuals and their wishes and worst of all common-sense.

There are rollers provided for the purpose of portage, but their design leaves much to be desired. For a start, they should be recessed in the concrete – as it stands, they can easily damage a boat coming up to them. There is a winch at the top, but the handle must be worked by an Anglian Water Authority minion, who should be telephoned etc. Pity they do not do an R.T. kit for a Mirror dinghy!

Having struggled to the top of the barrage we paused to take in the sight of the last lap. The tide was well on its way out, but sufficient to take us to Manningtree. After a very awkward launch at the rollers, we set the headsail and made for the railway bridge. Here at last I managed to reclaim some of my lost esteem over the mast lowering episode. Colin started to worry about clearing the railway bridge – British Rail would not be too pleased about a collision claim on the basis that an intercity express when crossing the Stour counts as a power driven vessel and as such should give way to sail.

However, with a "Don't panic Colin, I know these waters like the back of my hand" we cleared by at least half an inch and promptly ran aground.

Of course, this was an old gaffer's trick of steadying the boat while we set the mainsail. Slowly we slid across the mud and found the channel and within a few minutes grounded for the last time on the Stour Sailing Club hard.

After the refinement of Flatford, Manningtree on regatta day was a let-down. Most of the population were enviously drunk, too far gone to notice the making of a little bit of history!

But there was one couple, cooling off on the sea wall who got up and said, "What are you doing here – you're not due in till Sunday!"

So ended the epic. From being in the company of Chichester, Drake and Magellan, I returned to my normal duties as Mr. average man with family responsibilities and rats to catch. No sparkling champagne but a vigil with stick and traps which was to see me through the next day.

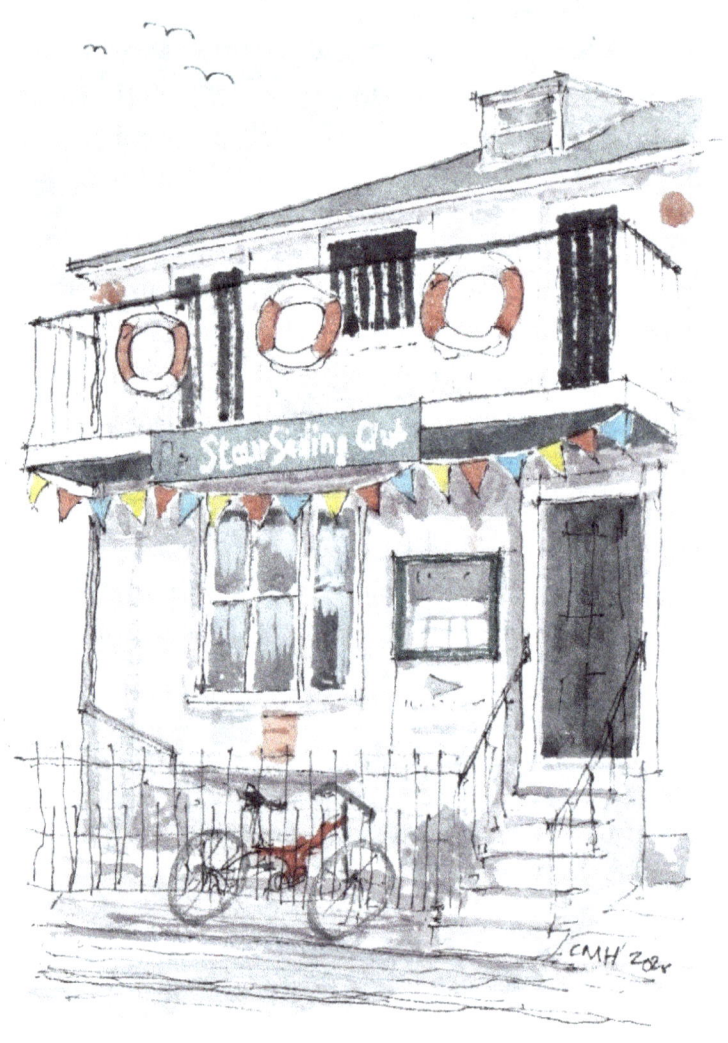

I hope the story does not end here. I am, in a sense, very disappointed in the dinghy sailing brethren that they have not even thought of such a trip, which surely give a greater challenge than belting round a couple of buoys for an hour. The voyage was, I believe, the first sailing boat navigation of the river in modern times, possibly ever. Paintings by Constable show lighters which although primarily horse-drawn had a small sail to help on down-wind legs. (They also show far less trees about to shield the wind)

But really it was not an impossible journey to make. Most of the river is in good condition, and only a few places require the lowering of a mast. Many stretches could give first-class inland sailing in the winter, far better and more interesting than many gravel pits and reservoirs.

In terms of the River Stour itself, it means that something bigger than a canoe can travel the whole length of the river. If the aim is to eventually re-open the river navigation to cruising boats (whether power or sail), the passage of sailing dinghies is the next step.

Perhaps an idea would be to have a rally involving a pair of Mirrors from several sailing clubs and a competition possibly sponsored by a local brewery!

A working waterway is far better than a disused one. The demand for amenity in East Anglia grows yearly, and the introduction of a fully navigable river into our overstretched areas of water-sport can only help. Proper locks, dredging, tow paths and even commercial applications can only improve the situation.

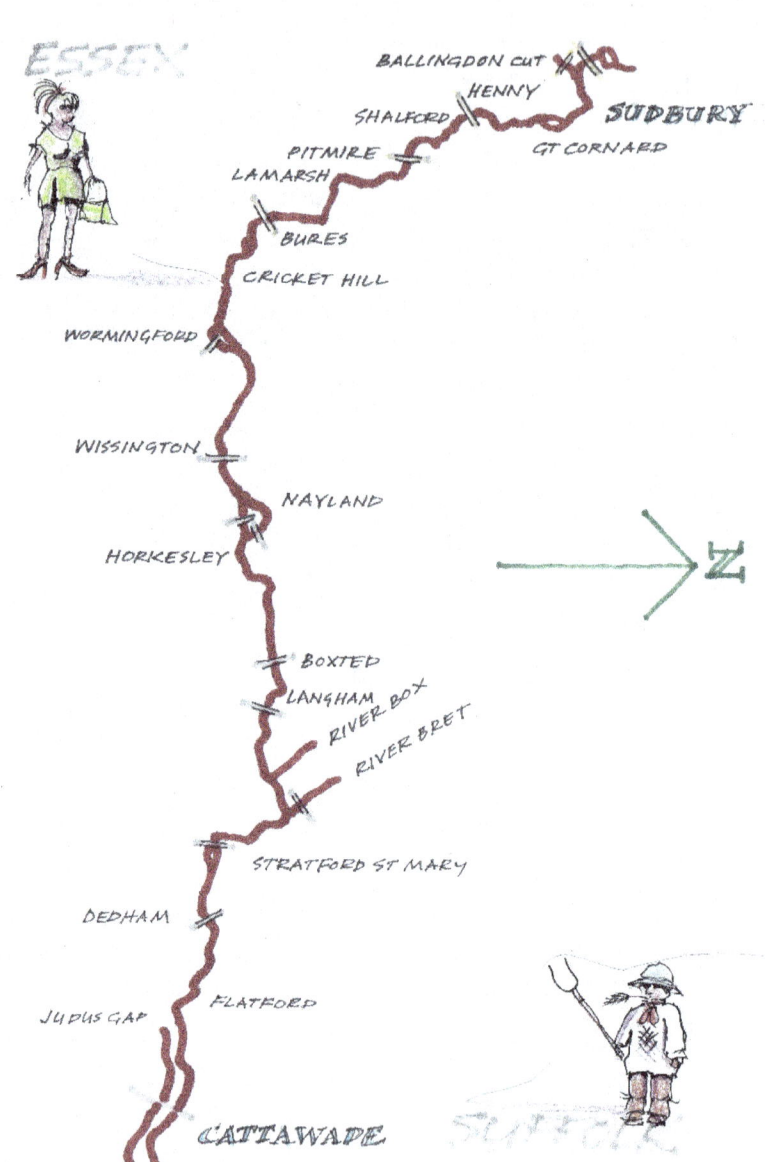

ESSEX

BALLINGDON CUT

HENNY

SHALFORD

SUDBURY

PITMIRE

GT CORNARD

LAMARSH

BURES

CRICKET HILL

WORMINGFORD

WISSINGTON

NAYLAND

HORKESLEY

N

BOXTED

LANGHAM

RIVER BOX

RIVER BRET

STRATFORD ST MARY

DEDHAM

JUDUS GAP

FLATFORD

CATTAWADE

SUFFOLK

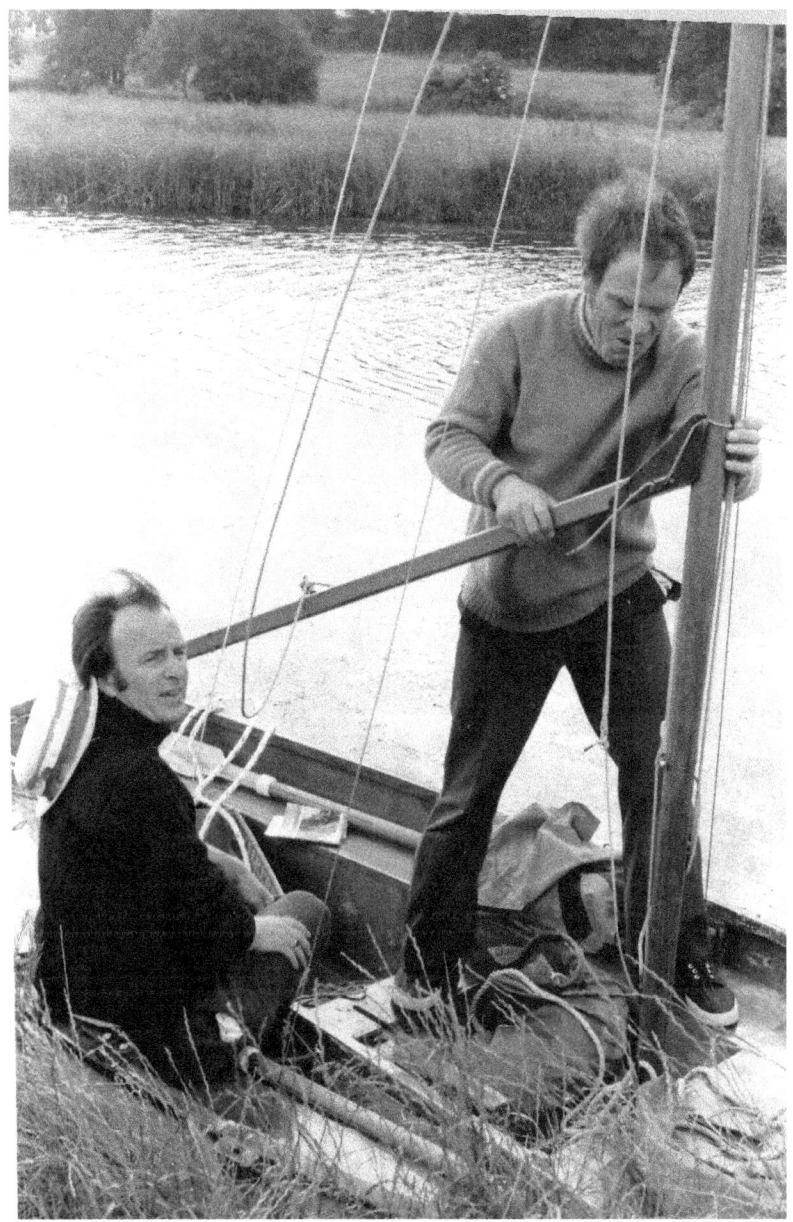

CHURCH TIMES August 17, 1979

Extracts from "Holiday questions of change & time"   By
Douglas Brown

*I have just had my big pre-summer-holiday tidy-up –
getting rid of twelve months' sludge of paper. It is
only when you retire from a big organisation and
start freelancing that you realise how much routine
tedium your secretary took from you. Without her I
find it impossible to flick through, let alone read, all
the stuff that comes my way – periodicals, press-
releases, and a good deal of pure (or impure)
propaganda.*

*But, after a lifetime in journalism, you do come to
know almost by touch what is likely to be useful at
once and what is not. So, I sling all the unlikely stuff
into a pile in the corner; and there, like Topsy, it
grows. When the time comes for it to be dealt with, I
invent all sorts of reasons for putting off the evil day.
At last, in an appalling temper, I start, knowing that
it would be even more awful when I get back, with
another pile waiting on the doormat. But, among the
mass of paper – so much from strange parts of the
world; and two abusive, unsigned missives, one
accusing me of being a Papist and the other the
lackey of Calvin – I found two copies of Lock Lintel.*

*Lock Lintel is the journal of the River Stour Trust.
The name comes from the many locks with their
gates and lintels of this river which divides Suffolk
from Essex and beside whose banks the painters
John Constable and Thomas Gainsborough were
born.*

The Stour Trust is, broadly speaking, dedicated to making the upper reaches of the river navigable again. Many of the members work away weekend after weekend restoring locks and basins and landing stages and generally clearing up and caring, to say nothing of arranging all kinds of social events to raise money and often frustrated by the heavy hand of bureaucracy.

Life being what it is, I have had little time to read their undertakings in detail; and the magazine joined the pile in the corner. But, flicking over the pages during this week's clean-up, I came upon an article called "Red Sails on the Stour," by one J. R. Wainwright. Something prompted me to read it. And so, I sampled one of the most evocative and delightfully written adventure stories to come my way for an exceptionally long time.

It was a story of two young men who sailed a ten-foot dinghy from Sudbury, Gainsborough's town, down to Manningtree – probably the first-ever to do so. Manningtree is where the river suddenly widens out into the vast estuary, with Parkeston Quay and Harwich on one bank and Shotley on the other. There was a time when heavy, horse-drawn barges made their way up to Sudbury, but their day has been long over. There are parts now that can hardly take a canoe. That is a measure of the achievement of the two young sailors. Moreover, the Stour here is often less than thirty feet across – little enough indeed to manoeuvre a sailing boat. In places it is overgrown, and there are weirs in plenty to be porter aged.

As the author says, how strange it is that, with much incident to offer, so many of our rivers are hardly sailed at all; and that dinghy sailing seems to consist largely of belting round a little triangular course on the open sea.

So, had I not paused a little in my frenetic getting-rid-of-the-sludge, I should have missed this enchanting essay of youthful adventure on a river which I, too, have known and loved since boyhood, reminding me of those parts I still have not had time or energy to explore.

THE RIVER STOUR TRUST

The River Stour Trust is a charity led by volunteers dedicated to the restoration and conservation of the River Stour Navigation for the benefit of the public.

The River Stour is one of the earliest statutory rights of Navigation following an Act of Parliament in 1705 making it navigable from Sudbury, Suffolk to Manningtree, Essex. For generations, the River Stour has occupied a central position for many people on its banks, both in work and play. It is one of the most attractive rivers in the country, winding through a wide pastoral and wooded valley past towns and villages of great beauty and many historical associations.

We are proud that so many can enjoy this beautiful river thanks to the dedication and efforts of River Stour Trust members. Whether you are paddling or cruising, or simply walking or sitting beside it; there is an undeniable benefit of the river to our physical and mental wellbeing.

The River Stour Trust continues to work toward reinstating through navigation, to educate about the use and benefits of the navigation, to promote and share the river's history and future prospects, improve and retain river access points and campaign for a change to the byelaws to permit electric boats on the whole stretch of the River Stour.

The charity raises funds and awareness through annual events and educational activities on or near the river for groups of all ages and abilities. Our environmentally friendly electric boats comprise a restored Stour Lighter whilst we also operate a specially adapted boat suitable for wheelchair users. Our knowledgeable and enthusiastic volunteers enable visitors of all ages to appreciate Constable Country from the unique perspective of our river.

You can help whether you choose to join us as a member, make a donation, or simply support our activities and events to Preserve the Stour for Everyone.

www.riverstourtrust.org

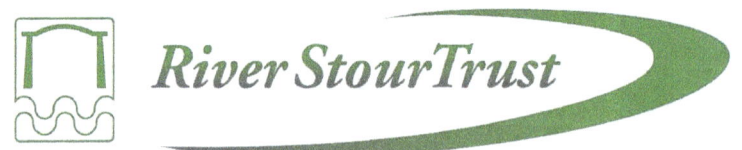